Ron Ransom Carves
AN AMISH
FAMILY
PLAIN AND SIMPLE

S0-AAC-462

Text written with and photography by
Jeffrey B. Snyder

Schiffer Publishing Ltd

77 Lower Valley Road, Atglen, PA 19310

DEDICATION

To the memory of Nancy Malan, who made the first trip to the beautiful Amish country of Pennsylvania with us and to my 87 year young father-in-law Pierce Bailey, whose quarter acre garden would make any Amish farmer proud.

Copyright © 1996 by Ron Ransom

All rights reserved. No part of this work may be reproduced or used in any forms or by any means--graphic, electronic, or mechanical, including photocopying or information storage and retrieval systems--without written permission from the copyright holder.

This book is meant only for personal home use and recreation. It is not intended for commercial applications or manufacturing purposes.

Printed in China

ISBN: 0-88740-893-1

Library of Congress Cataloging-in-Publication Data

Ranson, Ron.
      Ron Ransom carves an Amish family, plain and simple/text written with and photography by Jeffrey B. Snyder.
         p.   cm. -- (A Schiffer book for wood carvers)
      ISBN 0-88740-893-1 (paper)
      1. Wood-carving--Patterns. 2. Wood-carved figurines. 3. Amish in art. I. Snyder, Jeffrey B. II. Title. III. Series.
   TT199.7.R3567   1995
   731'.826--dc20   95-34653
                                          CIP

T 1325498

CONTENTS

Published by Schiffer Publishing, Ltd.
77 Lower Valley Road
Atglen, PA 19310
Please write for a free catalog.
This book may be purchased from the publisher.
Please include $2.95 postage.
Try your bookstore first.

We are interested in hearing from authors with book ideas on related subjects.

CARVING THE AMISH FAMILY

In keeping with the plain and simple life of the Amish, we are using plain and simple tools.

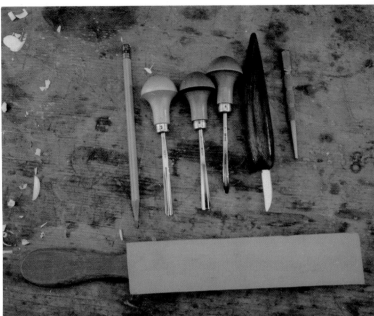

—LITTLE GIRL

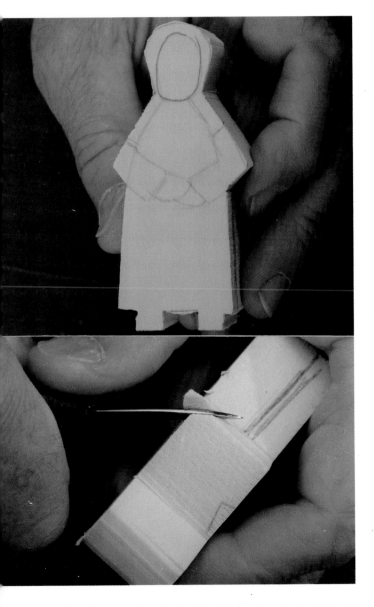

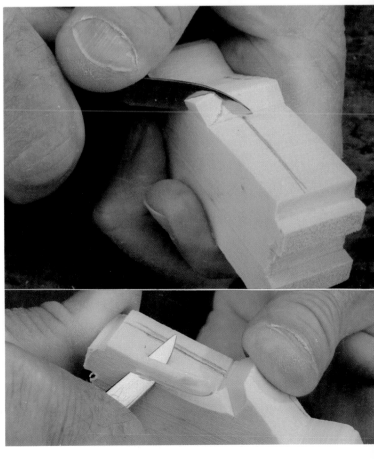

We will begin by carving the Amish children. Here is the little girl. Using a carving knife. start by cutting the back of the arms on each side of your bass wood block. For the Amish family, my bass wood blocks are 1" wide or less.

Begin rounding the back of the dress.

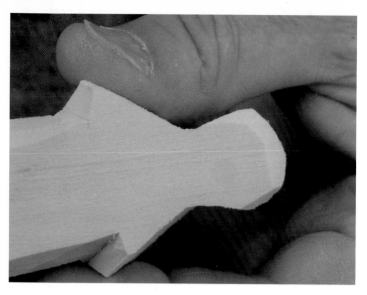

Starting to round the back of the head as well.

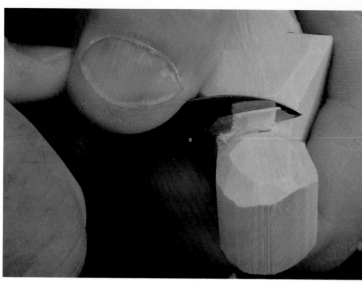

... then angle back and take a chip out from the shoulders ...

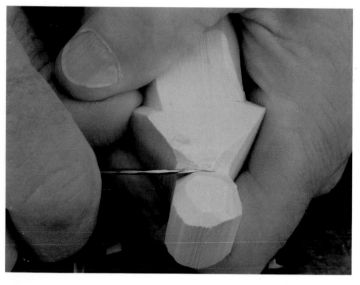

Make a series of V cuts to begin to round the back of the bonnet down near the shoulders.

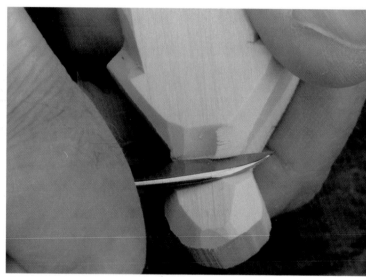

... and come back with an angled cut from the bonnet side. Now you are rounding with V cuts.

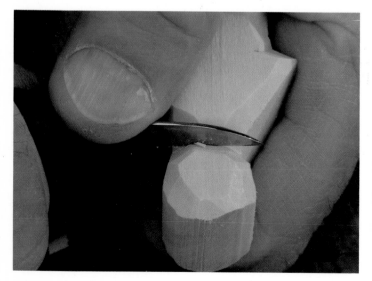

To make the V cut, rock the knife back and forth behind the head ...

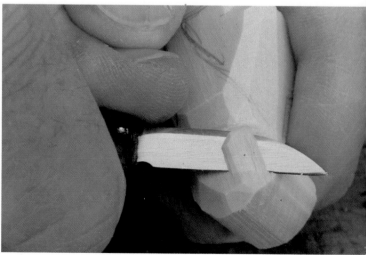

I have found that the bonnet is too big, so we are going to remove some from each side.

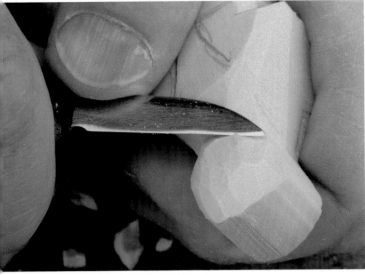

Continue to round the bonnet.

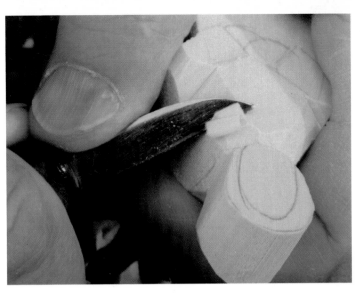

Begin to shape the body up into the head area.

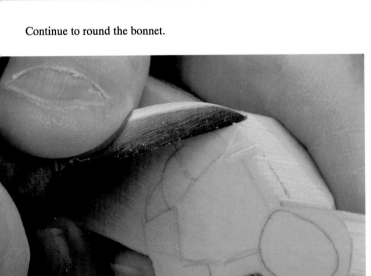

I am going to start working on the front now. Begin by removing a chip where the arm comes across the body.

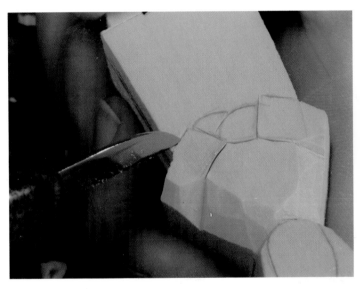

The hands will rest across the body. Incise the hands and arms now.

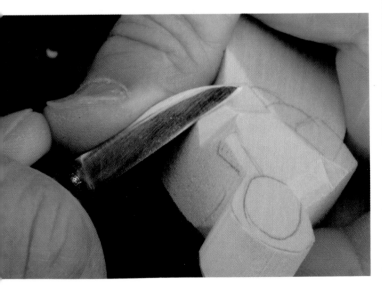

Do the same on both sides.

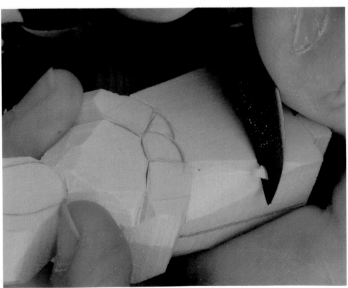

Shape the apron up into the arms and hands.

7

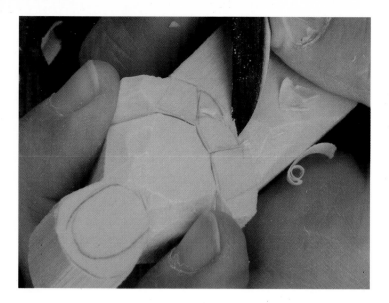

Carefully cut in with the point of the blade to define the hand area.

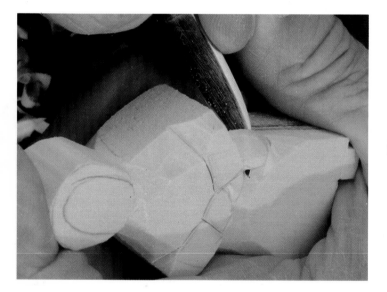

Repeat this process on the other side.

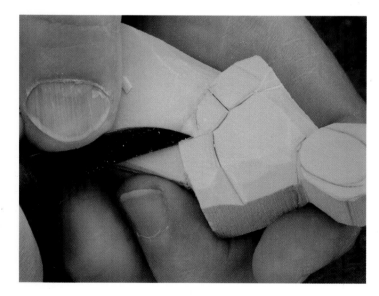

The left hand goes into the sleeve and is carved slightly under the right hand, which is on top.

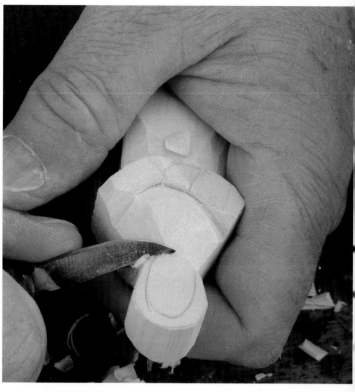

Round the chest area up into the head.

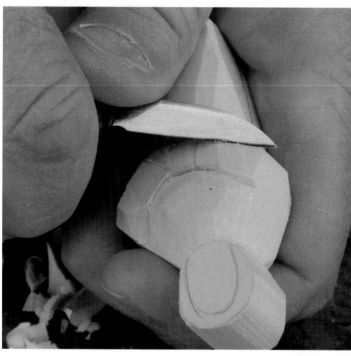

The arms are sticking out grotesquely. Begin to round them down. I am starting with the right arm.

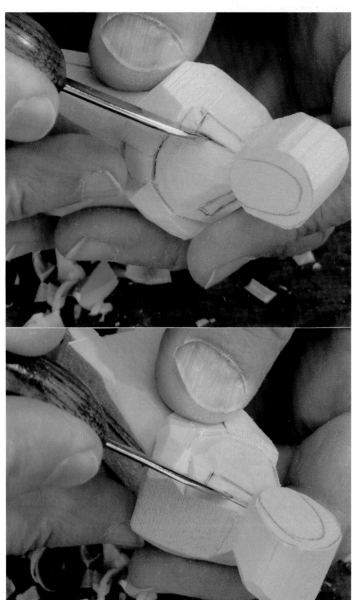

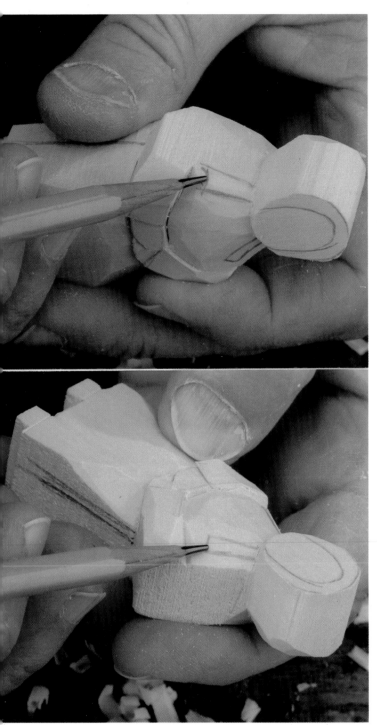

I have drawn in the bonnet sashes on both sides.

Incise both sashes lightly.

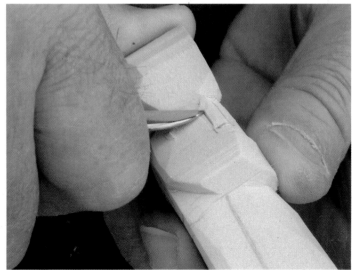

With just the point of your blade, come back and relieve a very small sliver of wood from around the sashes.

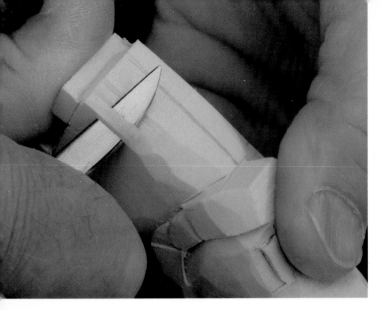

Continue to round the bottom of the apron on both sides.

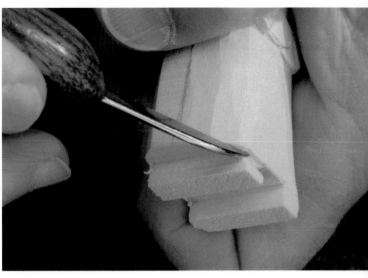

Then come back at an angle and take out a little chip. Do the same for both shoes.

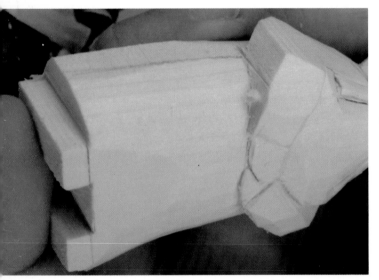

The rounded apron.

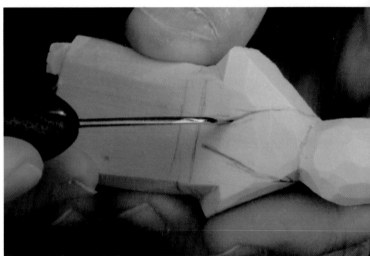

I have drawn in the apron from front to back. Incise the lines of the apron.

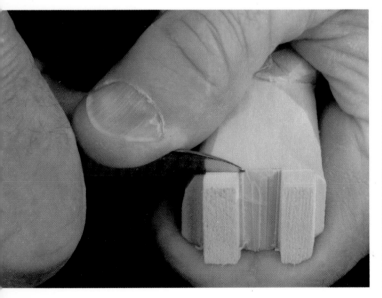

Rock the knife into the line where the apron meets the shoes.

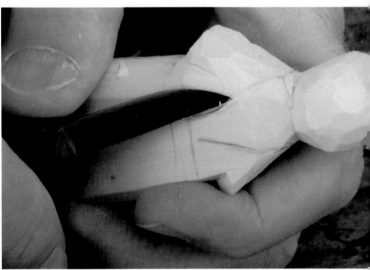

Holding your knife at an angle, cut up to the incised apron line.

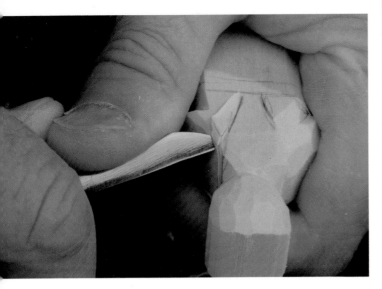

Repeat on the other side.

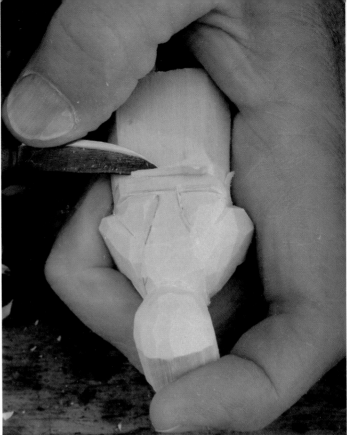

With the tip of the blade, take out a very small piece below the back of the belt. Cut up to the incised belt line.

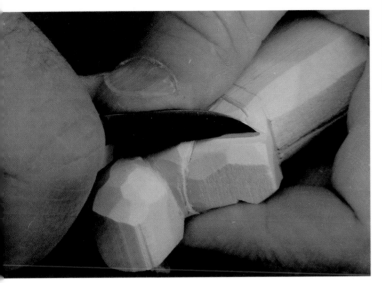

Make a series of V cuts on the back of the arm to give it more shape.

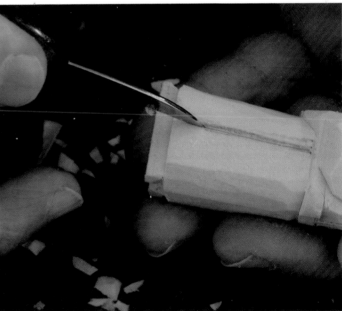

Draw in and incise a line where the apron and the dress meet. Incise the line on both sides of the apron.

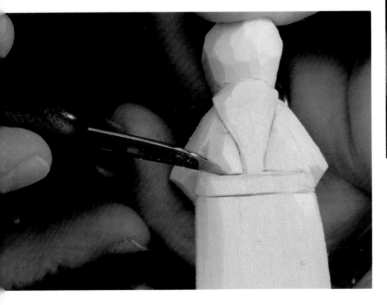

I have incised the belt along the back of the apron.

11

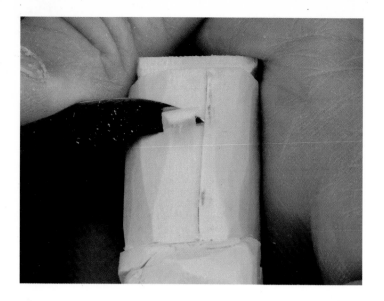

Lay your blade almost flat and go back along the line of the apron and the dress, taking out a very small piece of the dress.

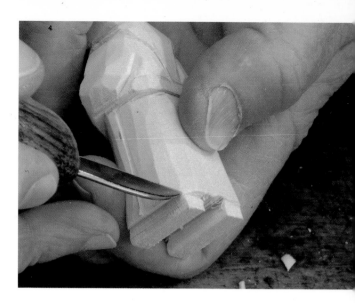

... don't cut in at an angle. Make your cut perpendicular to the bottom of the dress.

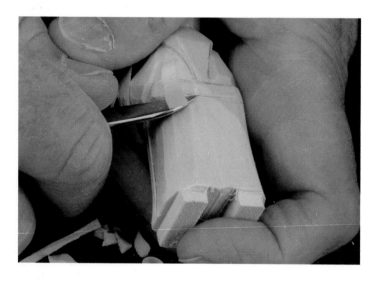

Go from side-to-side, rounding and giving some shape to the back of the dress.

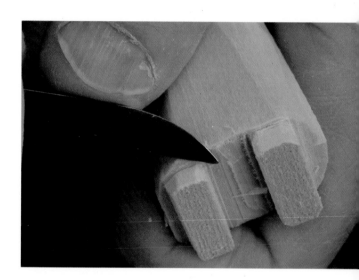

Gently round the heels ...

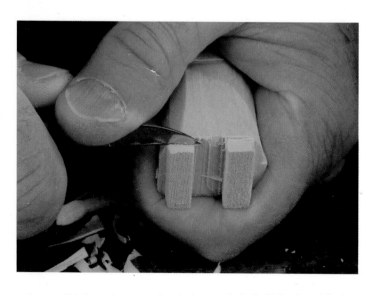

As you did along the front of each shoe, rock the knife back and forth along the back of each shoe, but this time ...

... and the toes.

12

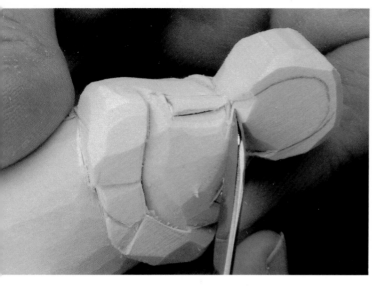

I have cut a little away from the bonnet at the side of the cheek.

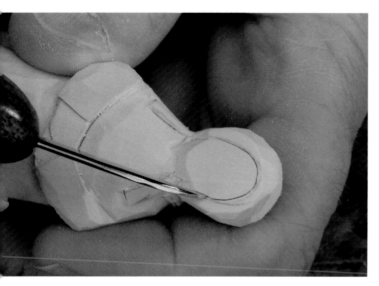

Draw and incise a line for the face.

Rounding the face. As I said in the introduction, to honor the Amish feeling about graven images, I am not putting any faces on these carvings.

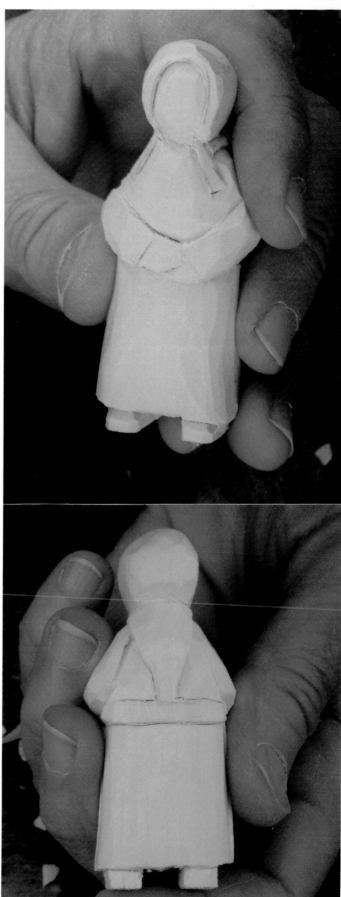

With a figure this small, you need to look at it closely from all angles and make sure you have removed all saw marks and that you have done any additional shaping that is needed.

—LITTLE BROTHER

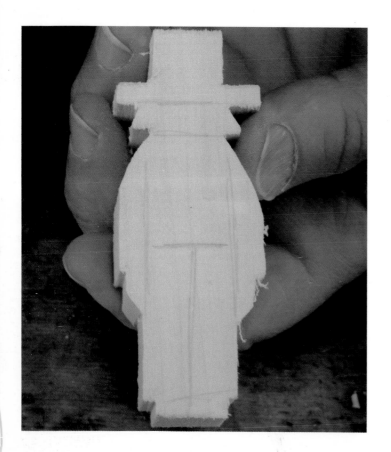 

Next, we'll carve our Amish girl's little brother.

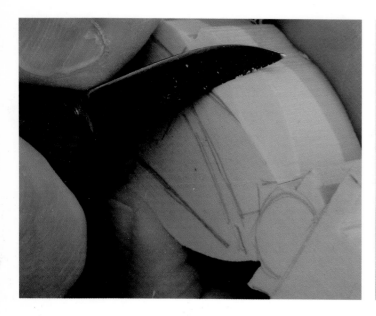 

Start by rounding the arms and the shoulders.

This is a good time to go ahead and incise the collar.

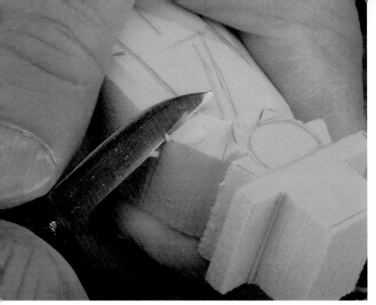

Rounding the other shoulder.

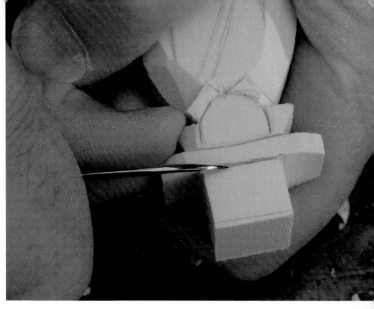

Make a deep incision along the line where the hat and brim meet.

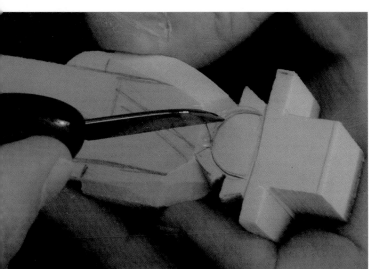

Draw in and incise a little round face.

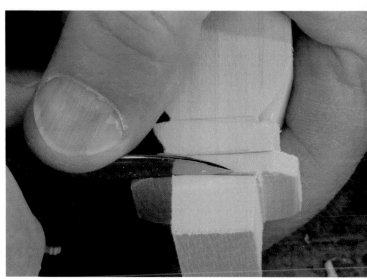

Make the same deep incision along the back of the hat ...

Begin carefully rounding the hat. This can be a weak area.

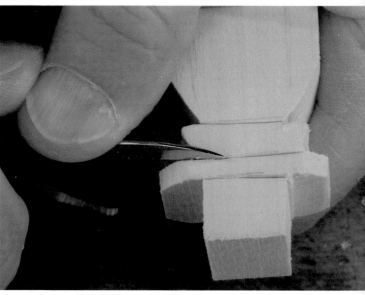

... and where the hat brim meets the hairline.

15

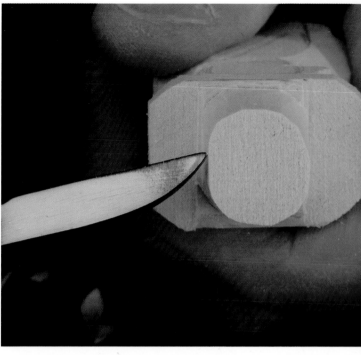

Start cutting away from the top of the brim to the top of the hat, ...

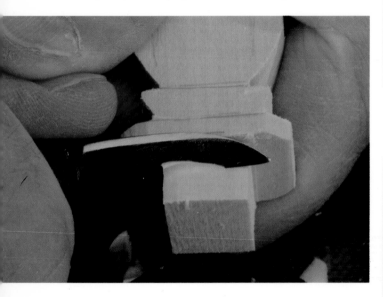

Look at the hat from above. When you are finished carving, the top of the hat should look nice and round from above.

... front and back.

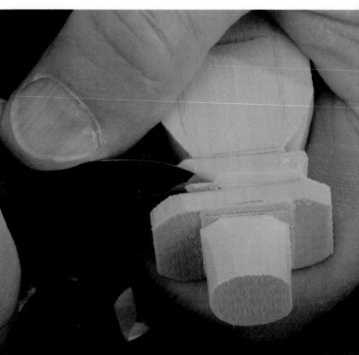

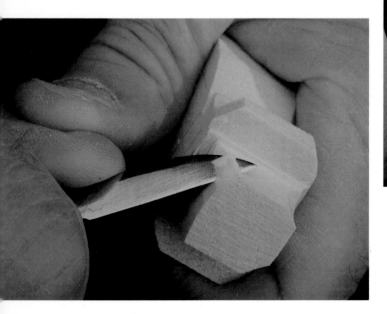

Carefully cut in where the hair goes up under the hat.

Round the corners of the hat as well.

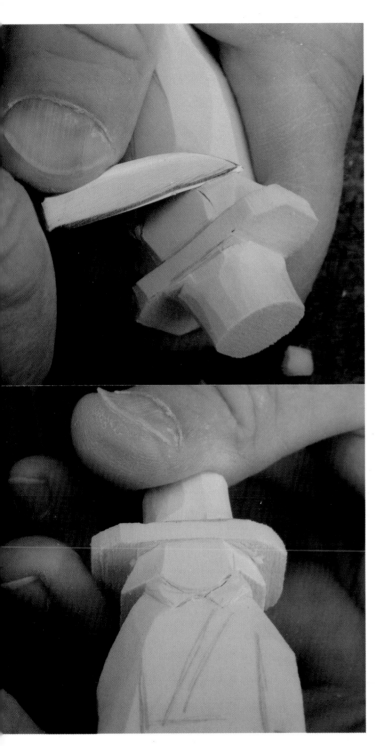

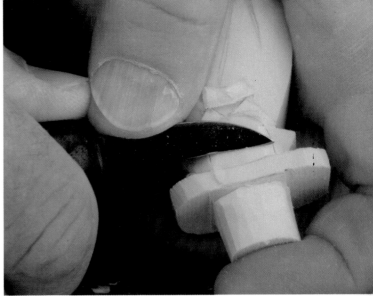

Round the forehead up into the hat.

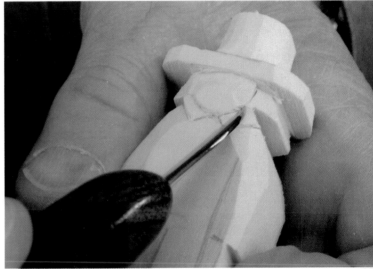

Now I see I am going to have to cut a little more hair away from the face to get the face to stick out as far as I want it to.

Angle the hair away from the face on both sides.

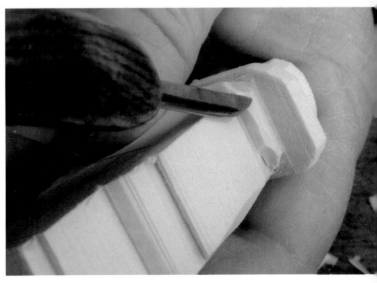

Further rounding back the hair.

17

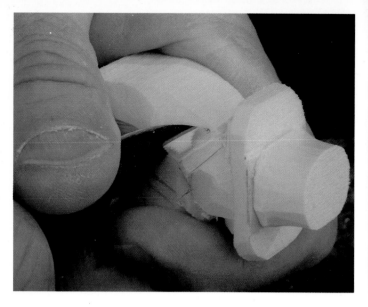

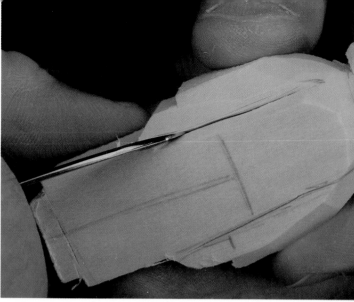

Now go back and continue to round the shoulder and arm up into the collar.

Incising the lines of the backs of the arms.

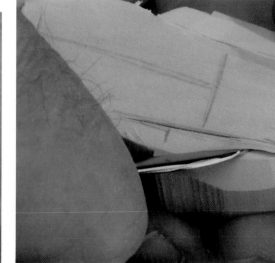

Start rounding the backs of the arms and shoulders as well.

I've redrawn the backs of the arms and sleeves as guides.

Cut in to the incised arm line at an angle from the outside of the arm inward.

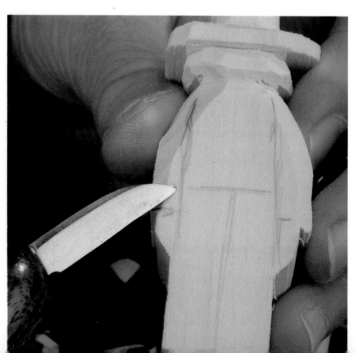

Then cut in from the back side at an angle and the center should flip out like this.

18

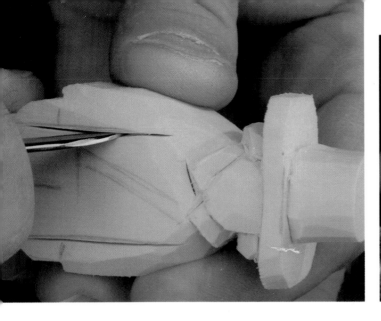

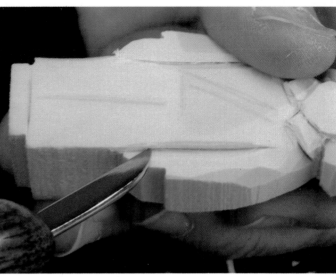

Repeat along the front of the arms, incise the arm lines ...

Repeat this process along both arms.

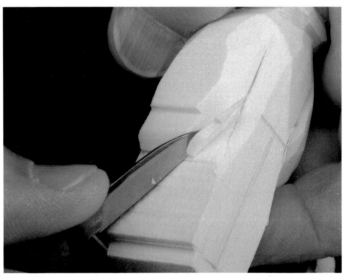

... cut in at an angle from the outside ...

On both sides, clip off a little from the backs of the arms to give them a more natural hang.

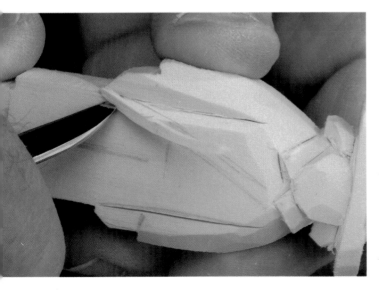

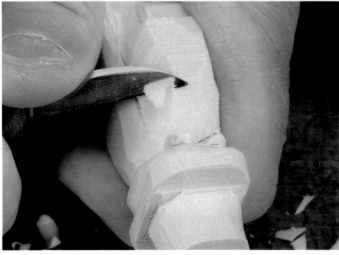

... and cut in at an angle from the body side, removing the extra wood from the center.

Continue to round the arms down, taking some of the excessive fullness out of the sleeves.

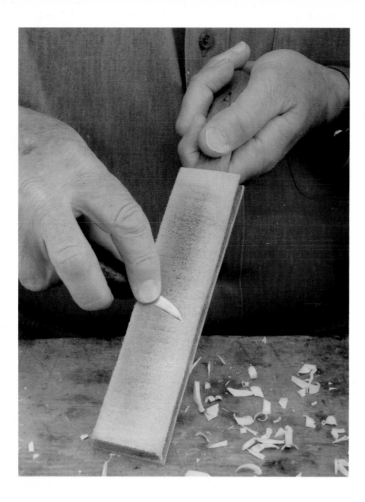

Take some time out to sharpen your knife. Fastened to the handle of this sharpening strop is a rough piece of leather sprinkled with aluminum oxide for initial knife sharpening.

Smooth leather on the other side of the handle finishes the job. This sharpening strop was made by my friend Pat Powers of Marietta, Georgia. I stop about every twenty minutes and hit my knife a few licks on this strop.

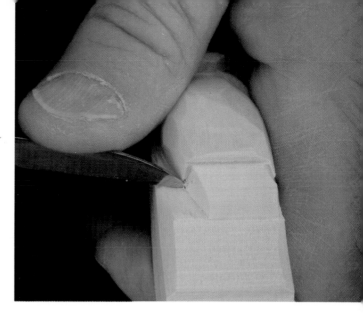

Cut away part of the hand where it goes into the sleeve.

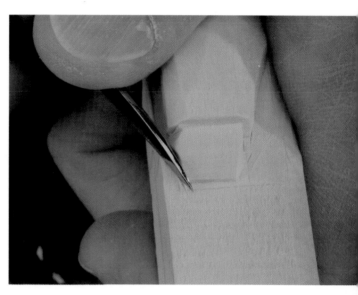

Trim a little off both hands to keep them in proportion.

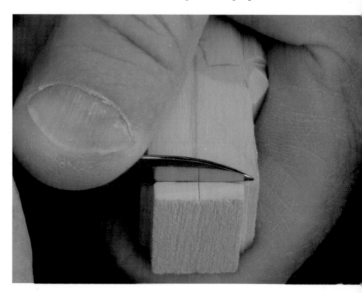

Press the knife blade in gently along the dividing line between the bottom of the pants and the tops of the shoes.

Cut back at an angle to give shape to the toe of the shoe.

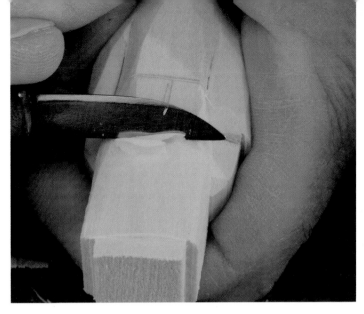

At the bottom of the seat of the pants, begin to round down the pants legs, moving from the seat downward.

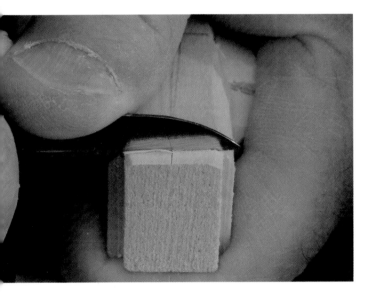

Repeat these steps at the heels.

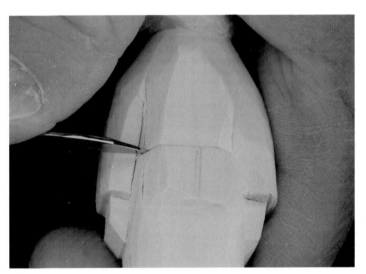

Incise the line at the top of his trousers.

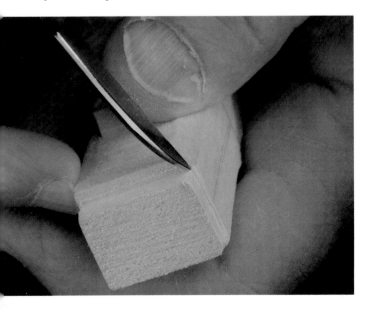

This time cutting back perpendicular to the line of the pants cuff.

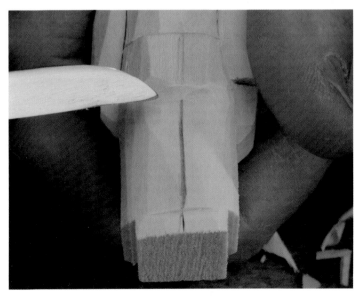

Redraw the line of his legs as shown.

21

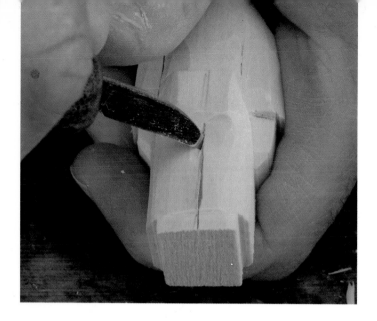

Incise the line.

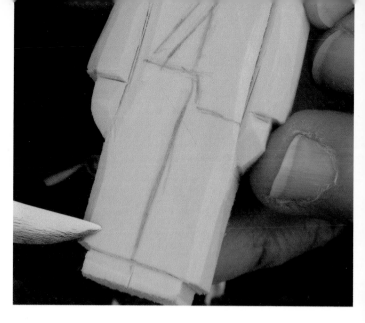

Along the front of the Amish boy, I have redrawn the pants line, the suspenders, and the shirt tail — which is now hanging out.

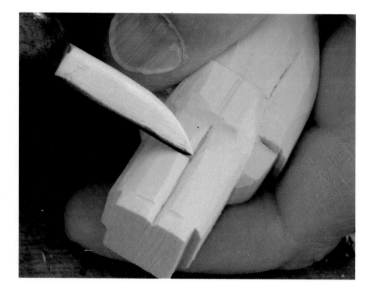

Cut out a V to give definition to the pants legs.

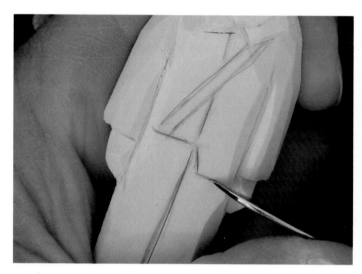

I have gently incised each of these lines.

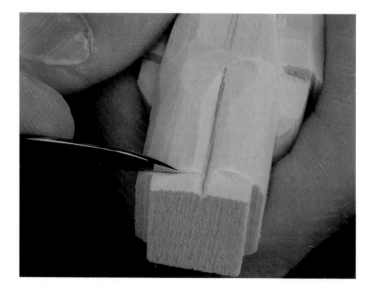

You will probably have to cut in the heel line again after the pants legs have been rounded down.

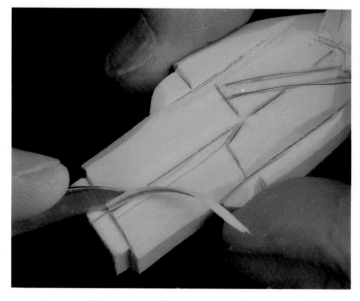

Take out the V shape between the legs all the way down to the shoes.

22

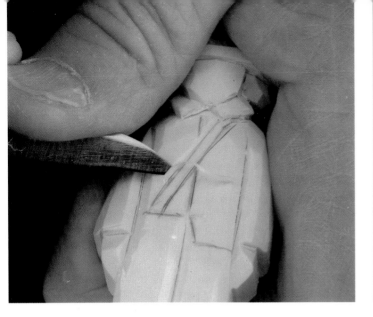

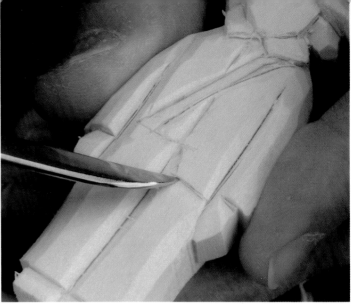

Using the tip of the knife, take out a very thin piece of wood along the suspenders line all the way down to the pants.

Where the shirt is outside the pants, undercut the pants below the shirt line.

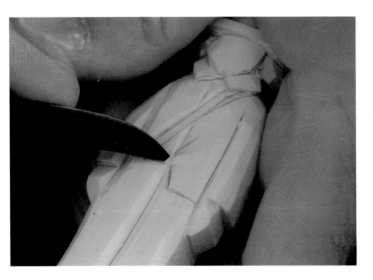

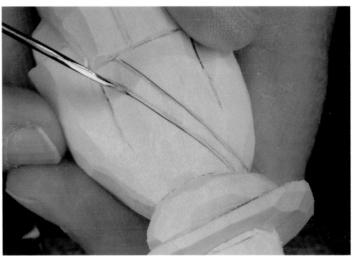

Take out a thin strip along the right hand side of the shirt only.

Come on around and incise the suspenders along the back.

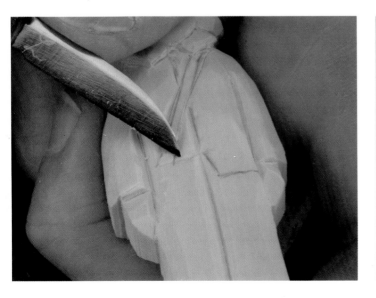

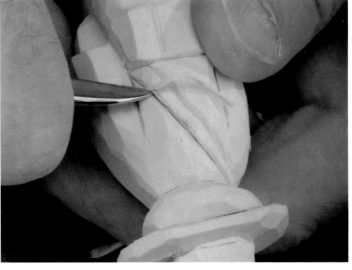

This gets a little tricky. The shirt on the right side of the pants is going into the pants. Undercut the shirt to show this.

Gently, with the tip of the knife, remove a small piece of wood along the outer edges of the suspenders.

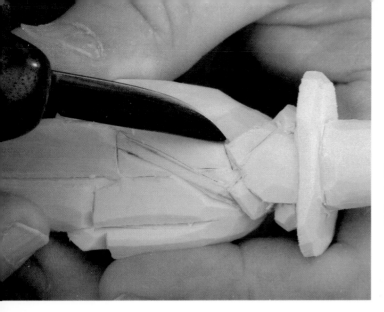

You'll notice we left the collar thick to start with, however, ...

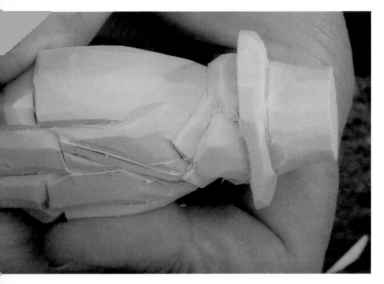

... it was much too thick. Trim some of it away.

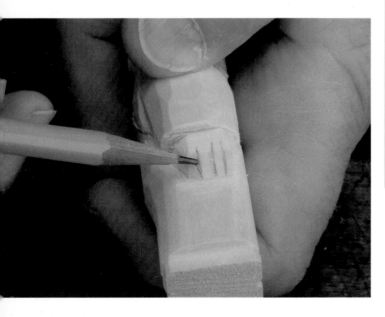

I have drawn in the hands.

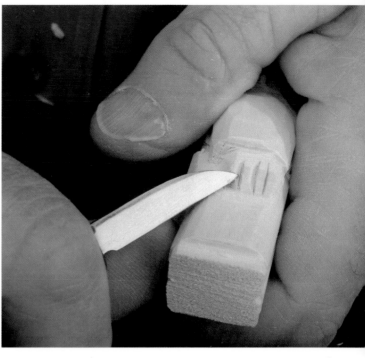

Incise each finger.

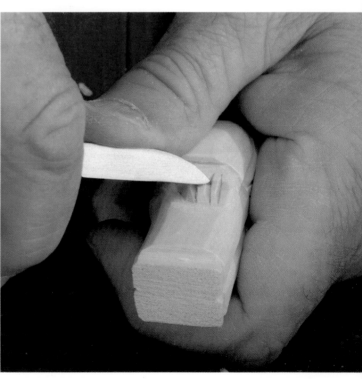

Come back along one side and cut a little angled piece out.

24

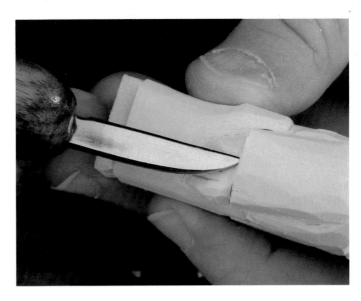

I felt the right sleeve was too big so I have taken some more off. This is a matter of personal taste.

As I said with the little girl, I am not putting any features on the faces in deference to Amish belief.

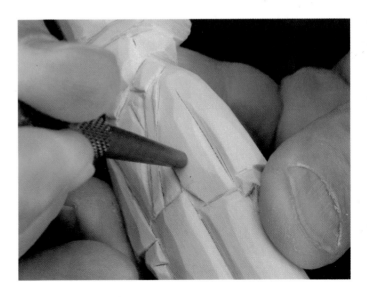

I use a small nail set to make buttons.

As with all little figures, look at this little boy from all sides to see if any excess wood needs to be removed.

This is the cut out for the Amish father.

Incise around the arms ...

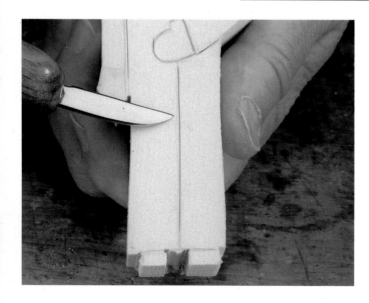

... and the pants legs.

Incise the backs of the arms.

Incise the line of the pants, from top to bottom as shown.

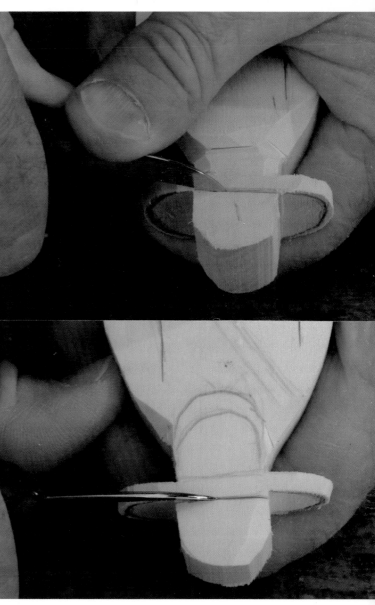

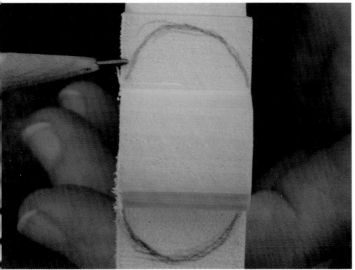

It may help to draw a circle around the hat before you begin to trim away the extra wood.

Incise the line where the brim and the hat meet, both along the back and the front.

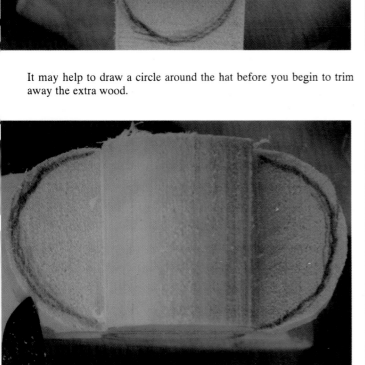

Round the hat down to these lines carefully ... or you'll have an Amish man with a derby.

Start rounding the hat.

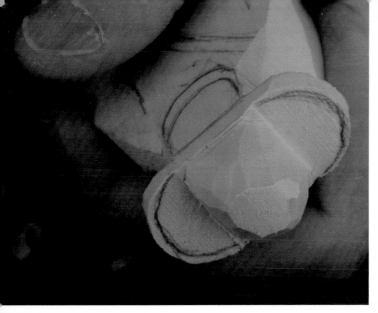

Keep rounding.

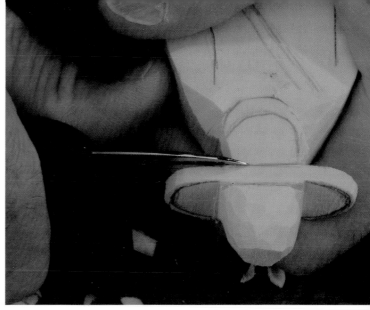

Deeply incise the line between the forehead and the hat brim.

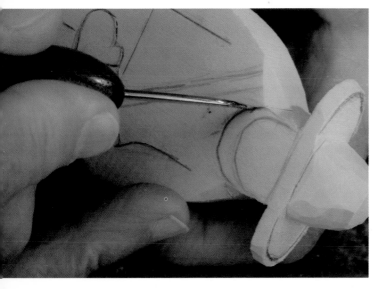

Incise around the beard. Amish men are required to wear beards.

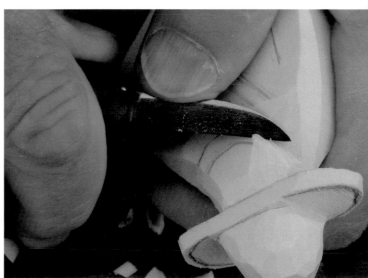

Start shaping each side of the face up into the hat line.

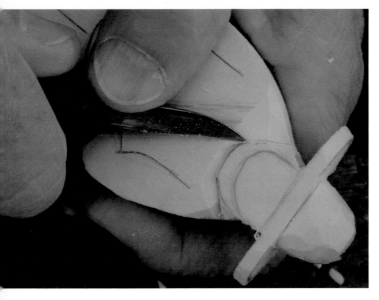

Then cut up to the beard, separating it from the chest.

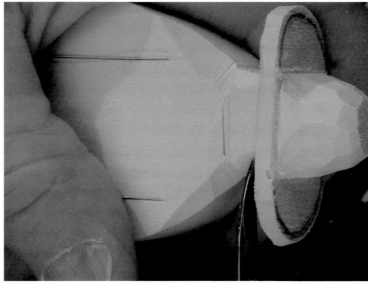

Repeat in the back, cutting the hair up into the back of the hat.

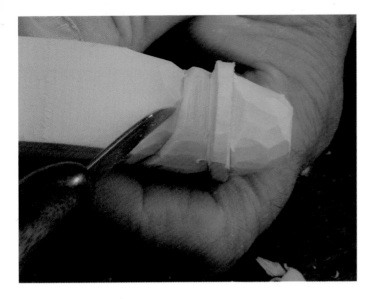

Cut a definite line where the hair, beard and shoulders meet.

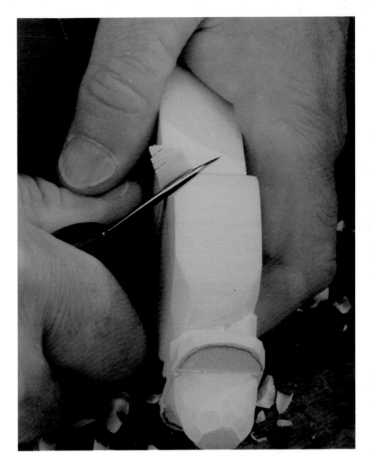

Leaving the head for a moment, start shaping the arms.

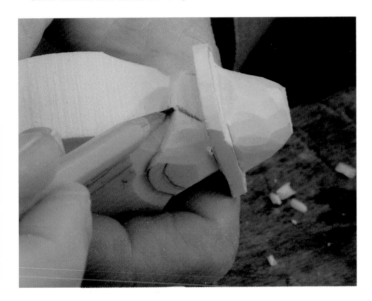

Draw in the hair line where the hair and beard separate. Keep both sides symmetrical.

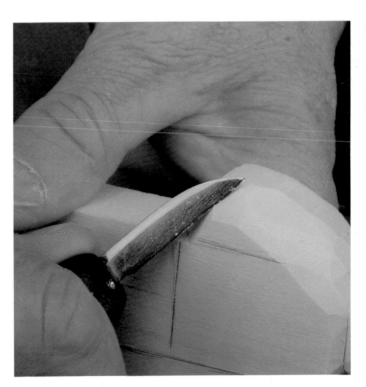

Continue rounding the arms.

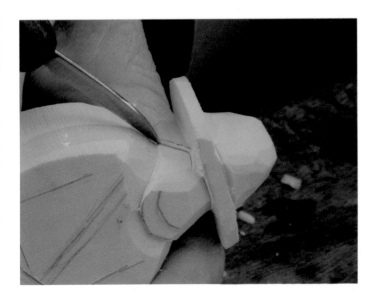

Incise this line and cut the face and beard down away from the hair.

29

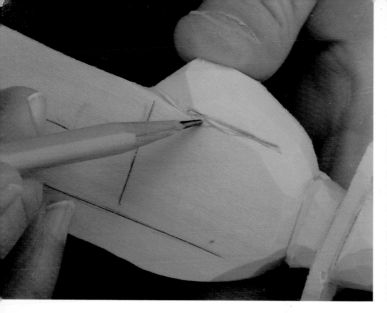

We incised the back of the arm earlier but have lost the pencil line while rounding the arm. Draw in the line again.

Trim away from his body to his left arm.

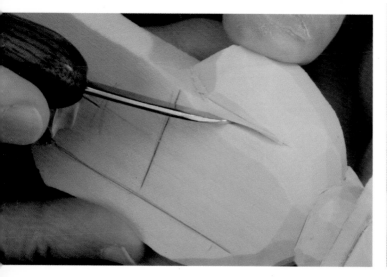

Incise the line of the back of the arm again if you need to. Cut in at an angle and remove a small piece on either side of the incised line to separate the arm from the body.

Add a couple of folds at the elbow.

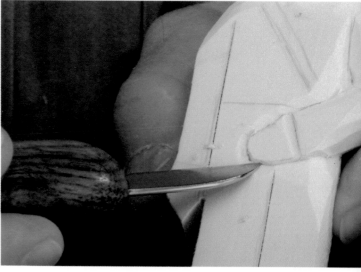

Incise the front of the pants up to the Amish man's hand.

Cut away from the hand where the hand goes into the sleeve and where the hand meets the trousers.

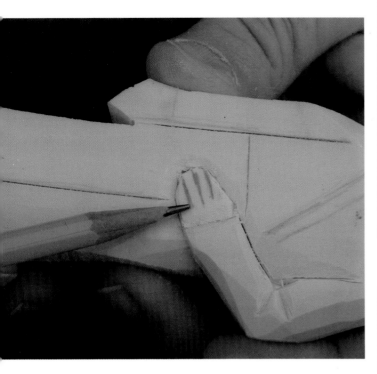

Draw in the fingers.

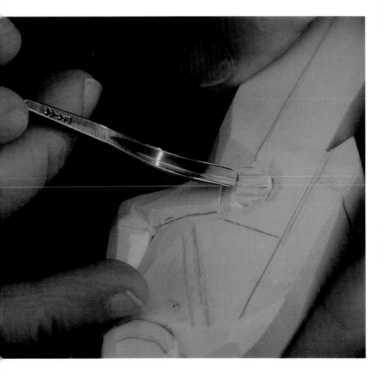

Cut in the fingers with a small V gouge.

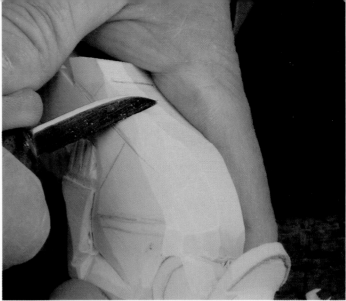

Rounding the arm and the shoulder.

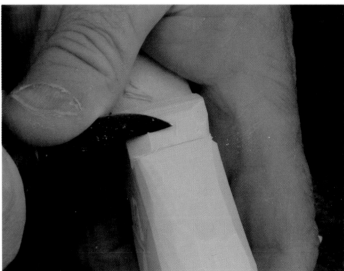

Separate the hand from the sleeve.

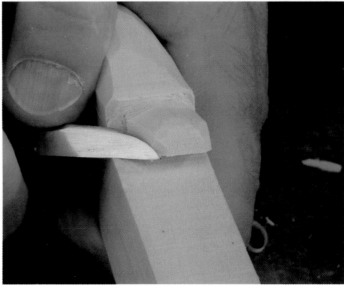

Trimming the hand to match the size of the other.

31

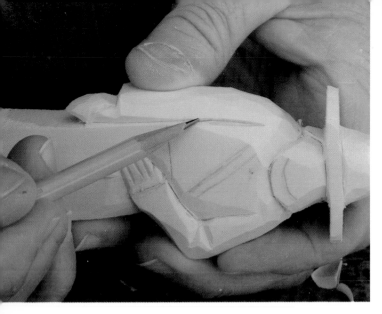

Draw the arm line back in.

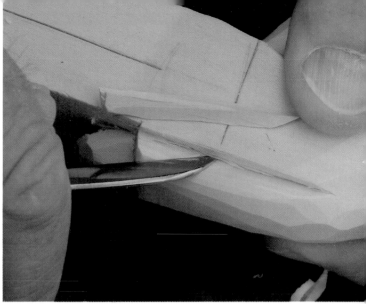

Cut out at an angle — like so — and that little piece between the arm and the body will pop right out.

Incise the line of the arm and cut out a little deep chunk between the arm and the body at the bottom.

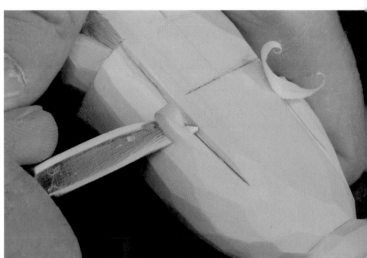

Continue to round the back of that arm.

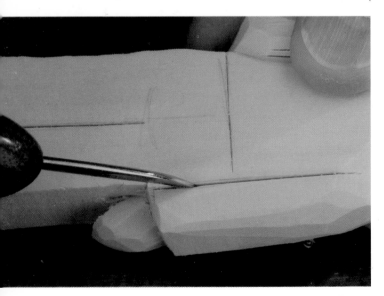

Incise the line along the back of the arm deeper now.

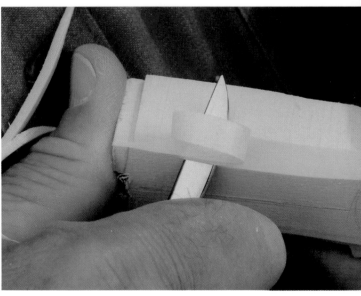

Round the outside edges of the pants legs.

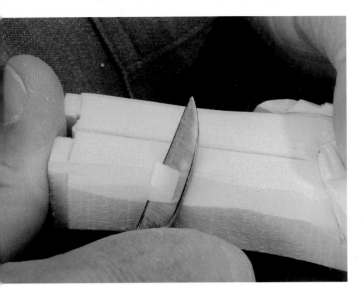

Continue rounding the outside of the pants legs.

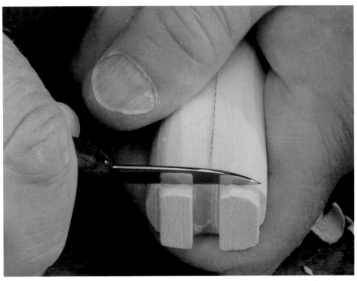

Lay the knife blade across the front of the feet where they meet the pants legs and cut straight in.

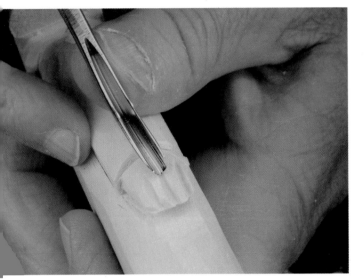

Cutting in fingers with a V tool.

Cut back at an angle to form the toes of the shoes.

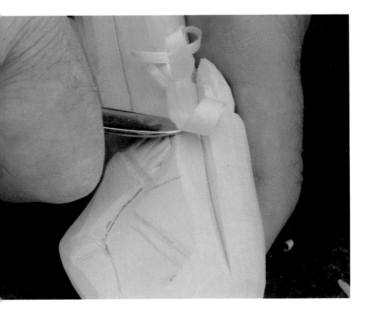

Round off the shirt and pants leg around the arm.

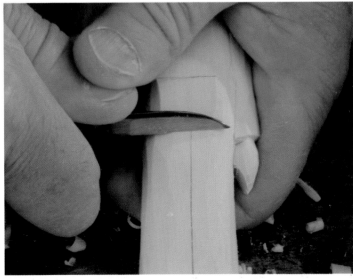

Go to the top of the incised line on the back of the trousers and make a rocking cut which will create a small rounding cut.

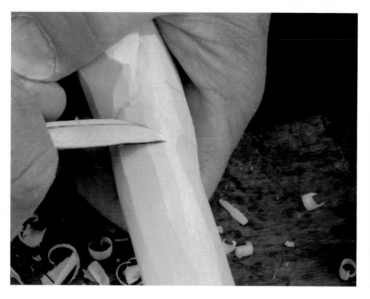

Like so.

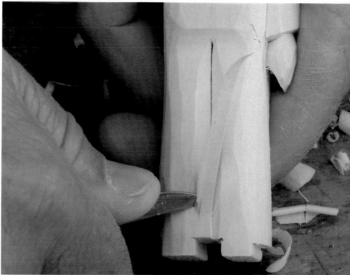

... and then on the other.

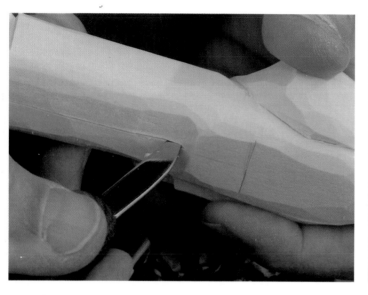

Go back and incise the back pants line about 1/8" deep.

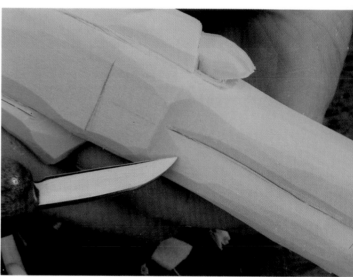

It should look something like this.

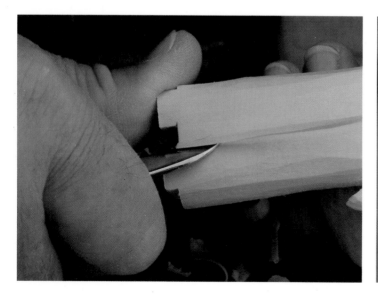

Come back at an angle and pull the knife down along the incision, first on one side ...

Round off any sharp edges along the back of the pants.

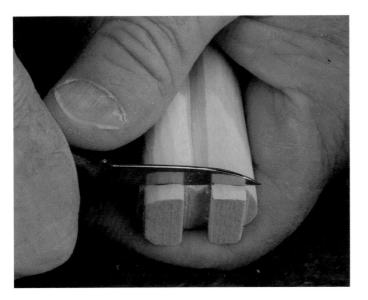

Now that we have the pants where we want them, we'll cut in the heels. First cut straight in.

Remember to make the second cut perpendicular to the pants legs and not angled as with the toes.

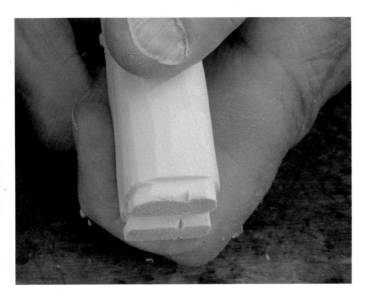

Notch the heels with small triangular cuts.

Incise the front of the pants as well.

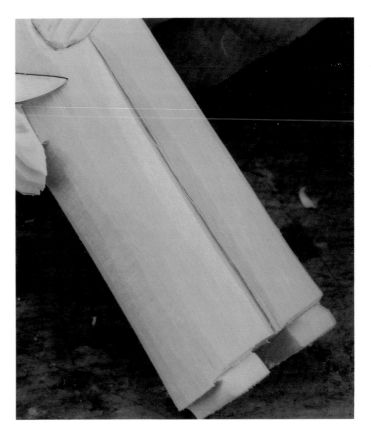

The incised front pants legs.

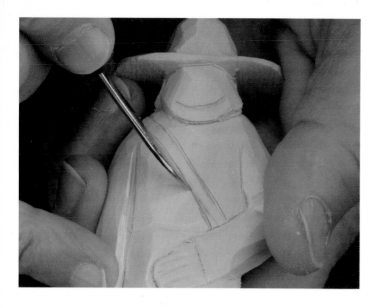

Lightly incise the suspenders.

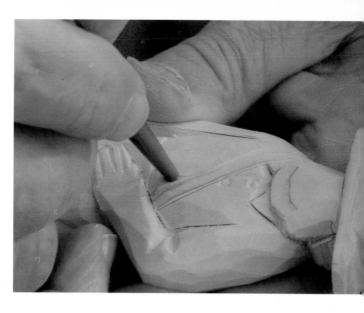

Put in the buttons with a nail set.

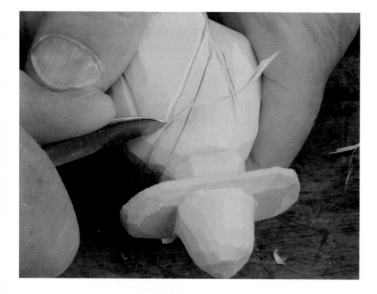

With the tip of the blade, go back lightly and remove a sliver of wood along the outside edge of each incised suspenders line. Remember this is just a suspender, not a money belt.

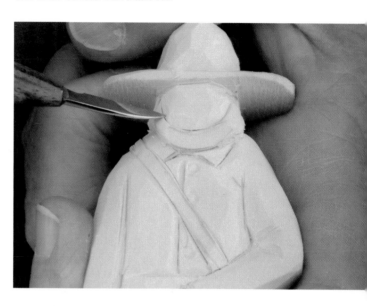

Incise the line of the beard and cut the face area away from the edge of that beard.

Clean away "fuzzies," soften any sharp lines, and you are ready to paint.

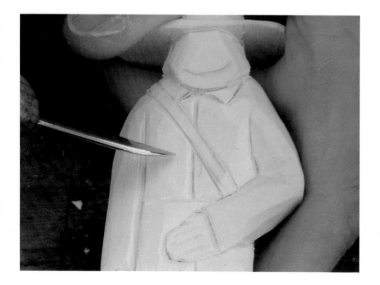

Cut in the collar and the front of the shirt.

The blank for the mother.

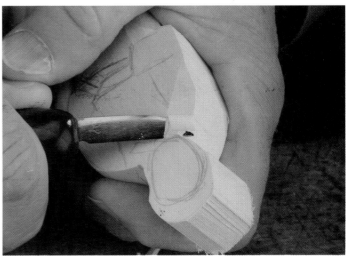

We want the mother to have nice soft lines, so we're going to start rounding all the sharp edges.

Round the arms and shoulders up to the head.

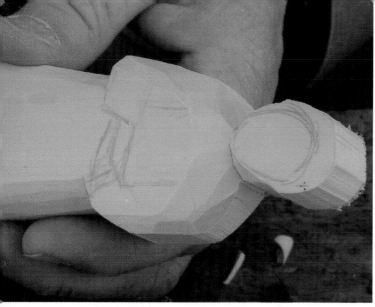

Both shoulders are rounded up to the head.

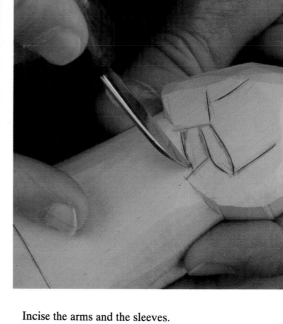

Incise the arms and the sleeves.

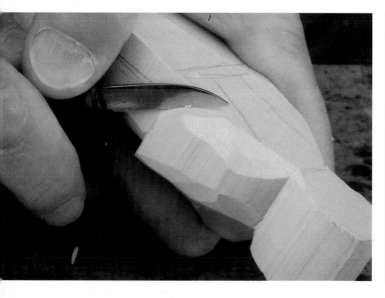

Start cutting in the backs of the arms to make them look more natural.

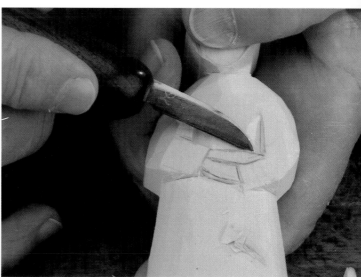

Cut away down to the right arm.

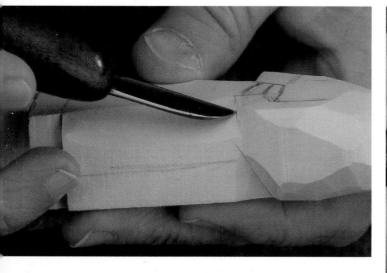

Notice that the left arm is further down on the blank. The reason for this is that the arms are folded and the left arm is under the right. The hands are not showing.

I have cut away up to the left arm (positioned underneath the right) as well.

Be sure that the arm that is underneath is cut back more than the arm above it for depth. This lower arm is in deeper than the overlapping arm above it.

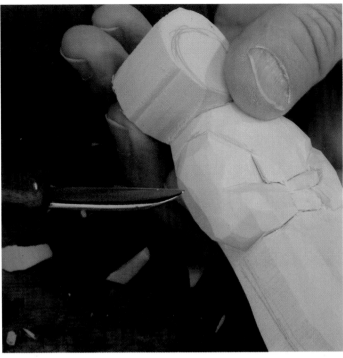

I have done the same to the right arm.

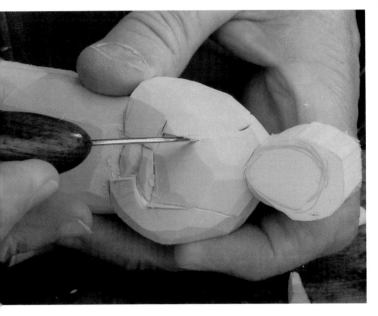

Incise the lines for the apron, front to rear, on both sides of the body.

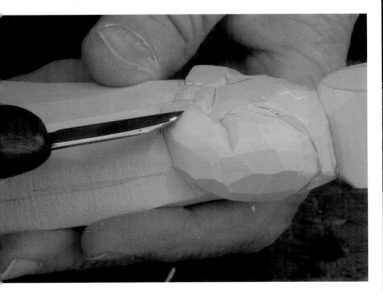

I've rounded and worked on the left arm to give it a more natural bend across the body.

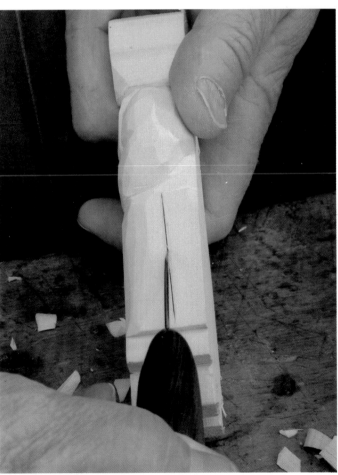

Make a healthy incision on the sides where the apron falls.

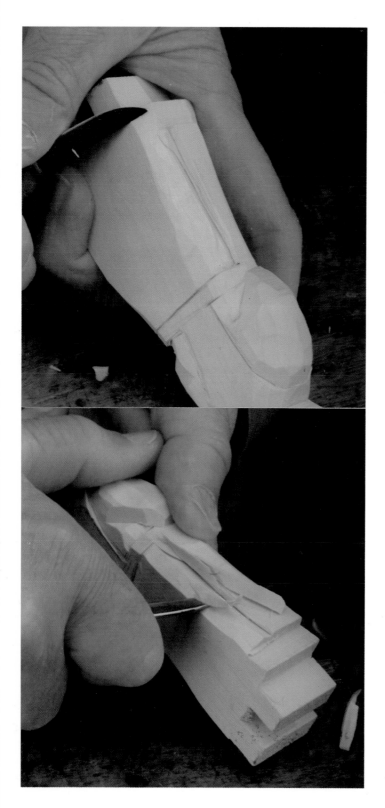

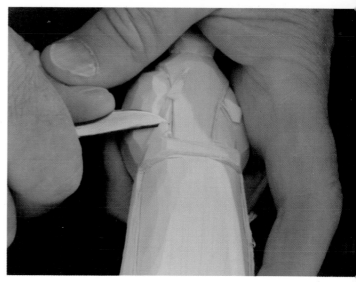

This is the line I have incised and trimmed away from for the back of the long apron. Cut down the sides of the apron along the back down to the apron belt.

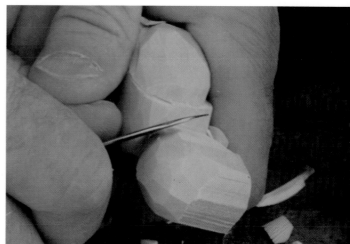

Rounding the bonnet.

Go back and trim up to the incised line of the back of the apron.

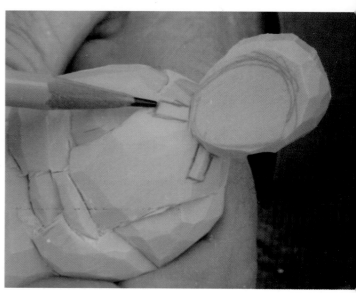

I've drawn in the bonnet ties.

40

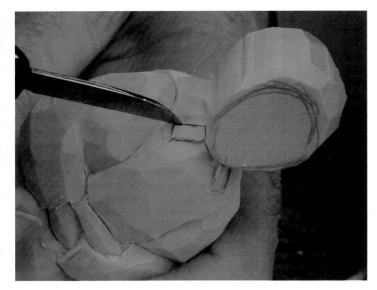

Incise and trim away around the bonnet ties.

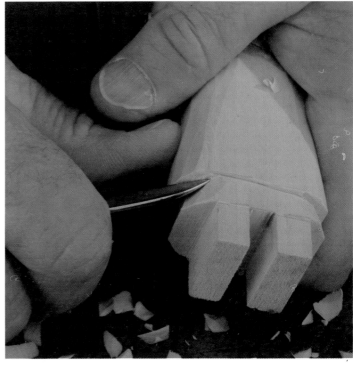

I have cleaned out the area where the dress meets the apron.

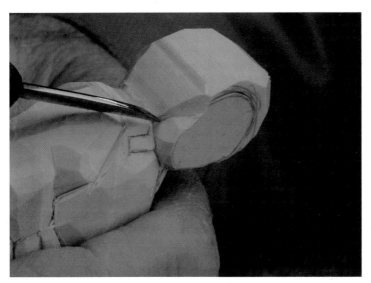

Angle the bonnet away from the face on each side.

Draw in some guidelines for the feet.

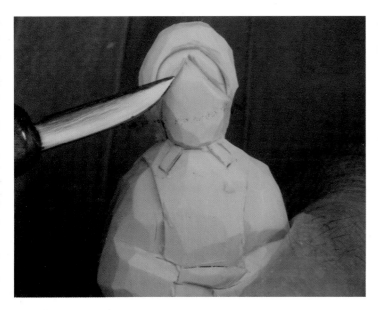

Draw in, incise, and cut the face away from the hair line.

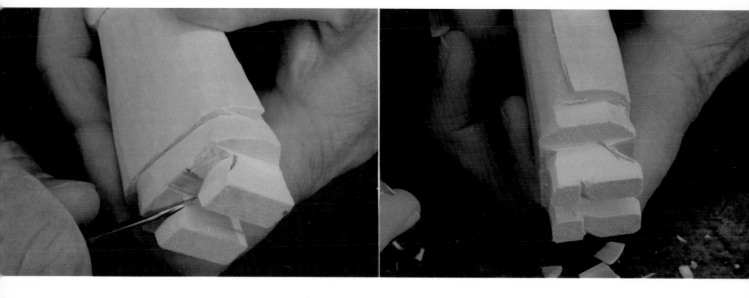

Cut away to the guidelines for the feet.   Round the feet and cut in the heel lines.

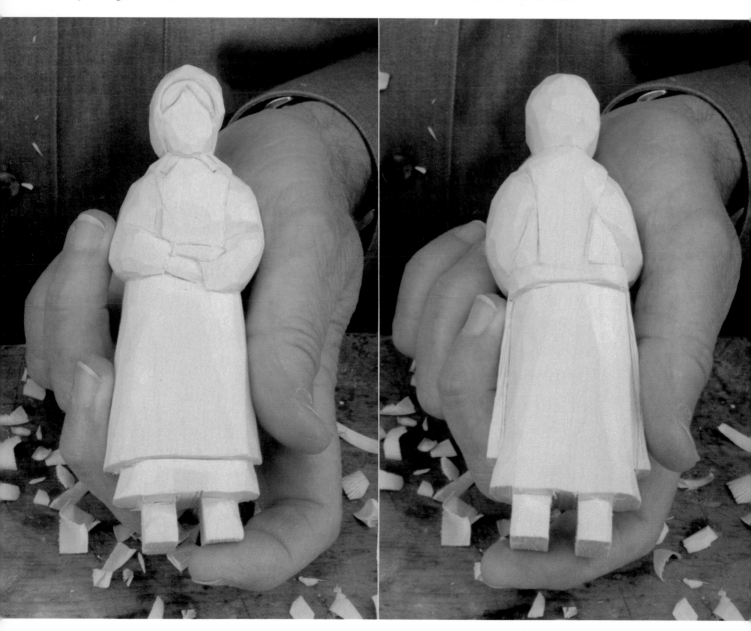

Go back and round any sharp lines you may have missed and clean up the saw marks. The Amish mother is finished.

—GRANDFATHER

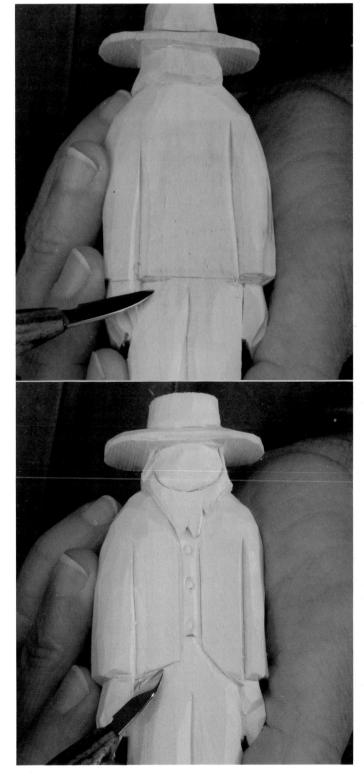

Here is the grandfather. The only major difference between him and the father is that grandfather has on his Sunday best.

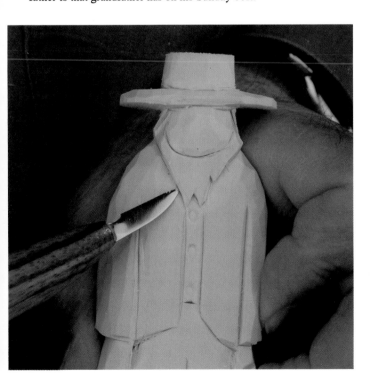

As he has gotten older, grandfather's beard has gotten scraggly.

Notice also that his coat has no lapels in front and is long in the back. When we paint, you will see that his coat is all black.

PAINTING THE CARVINGS

The colors we are going to use to paint the Amish mother are Black, Lilac Dusk, White, Blue Jay, Flesh Tone, and Brown.

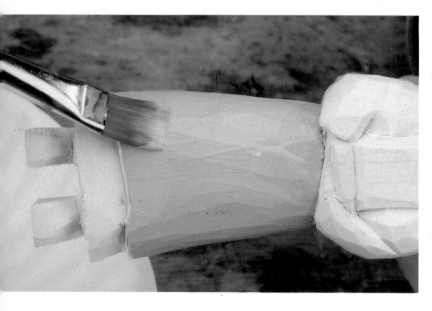

Painting the apron with Blue Jay.

Remember to paint the back of the apron with Blue Jay as well.

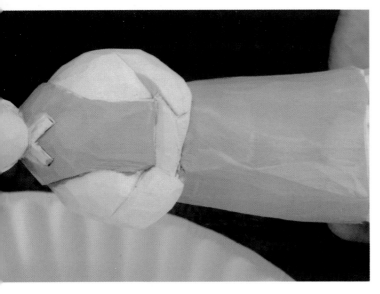

The painted apron.

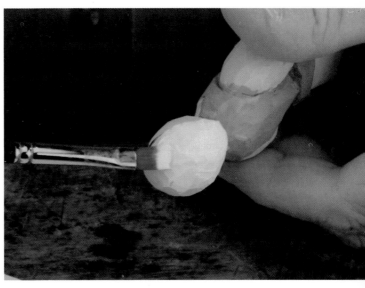

Painting the bonnet white.

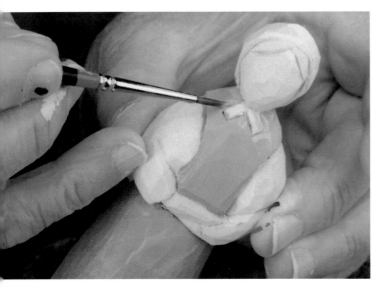

This little brush works well for the fine details.

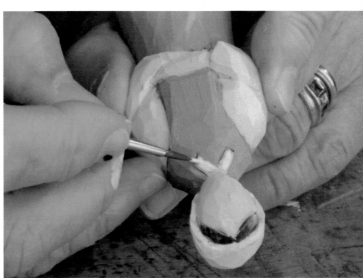

Don't forget to paint the bonnet ties white as well.

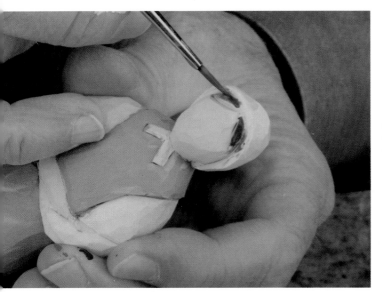

Putting in a little dab of Brown for the hair.

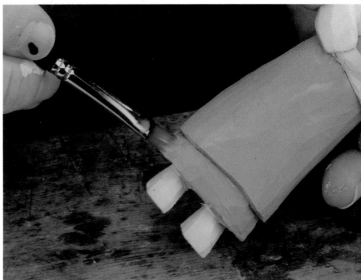

Painting the dress in Lilac Dusk.

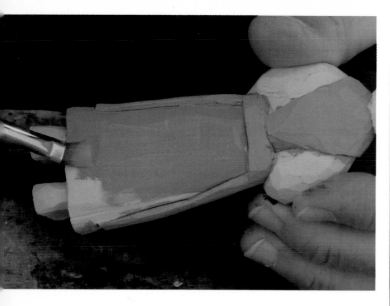

Continuing around the back of the dress.

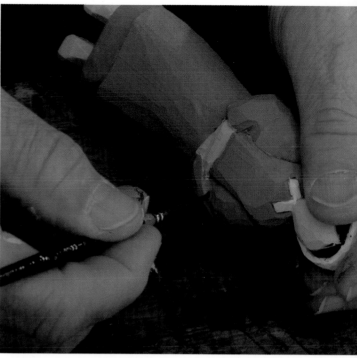

Using a small brush to touch up the sleeves.

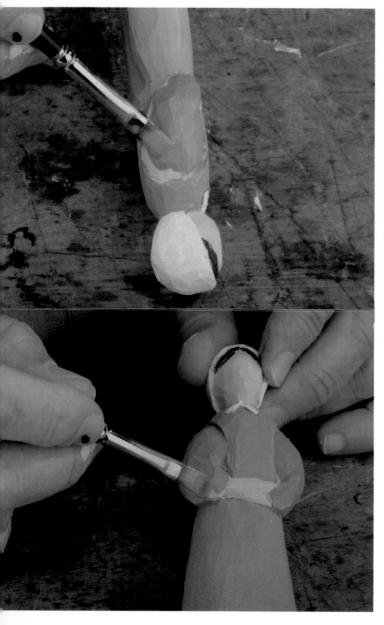

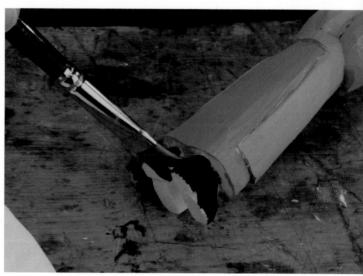

Painting the shoes black.

Painting the sleeves in Lilac Dusk.

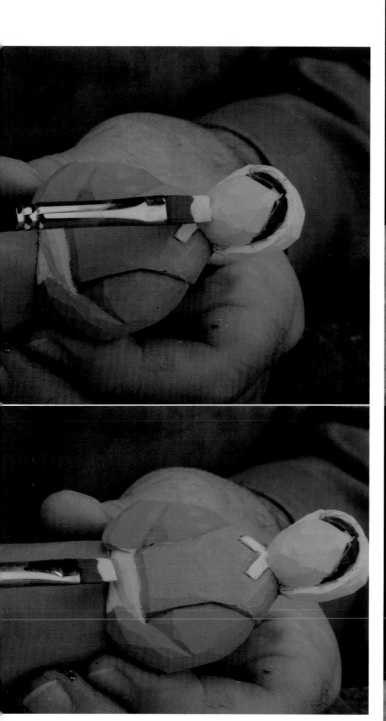

Use Flesh Tone on the face and arms. Be careful, basswood and Flesh Tone are very similar in color. If you leave a bare spot and "antique" the figure, that bare spot will turn dark.

The figure on the left has been "antiqued," the one on the right we just finished painting.

For the father, the shirt is Liberty Blue, the skin is Flesh Tone, and the buttons are White. The hat, suspenders, trousers, and shoes are all Black. His beard is Brown Velvet.

The boy is painted with a Bonny Blue shirt, Old Parchment hat, Black trousers and suspenders, and Flesh Tone skin.

The boy with his arm down has a Christmas Green shirt, White buttons, Toffee Brown hair, Black hat, suspenders, trousers, and shoes, and a Flesh Tone face.

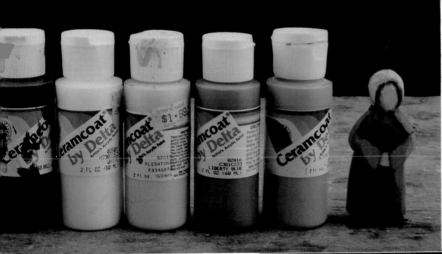

The little girl. The dress is Lilac Dusk, the apron is Liberty Blue, Flesh Tone skin, White bonnet, and black shoes.

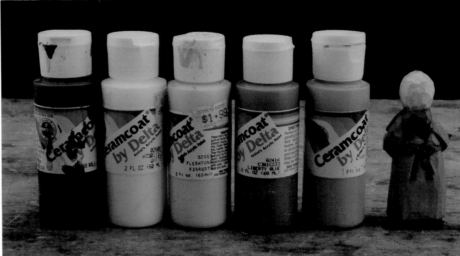

The grandfather. Flesh Tone for the face and hands, White for the shirt and beard, and Black for the hat, jacket, pants, and shoes.

These are the products I use to create an antique finish. If you have some other method, continue to use it.

This is important — spray your painted, dry carving with Krylon 1301 acrylic coating.

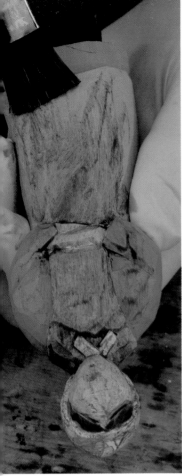

Cover the piece with a coating of Antique Mahogany Briwax. P.S. I am not dead, I am wearing a rubber glove to protect my hand.

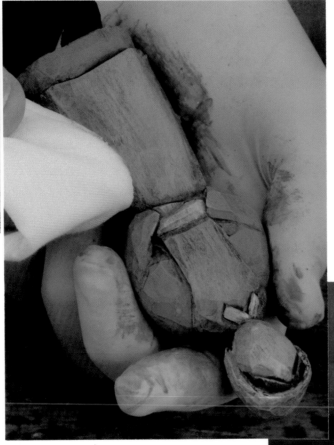

Take a soft cloth T-shirt or a cloth diaper and wipe off with neutral Briwax polish.

The finished Amish mother with a nice antique patina.

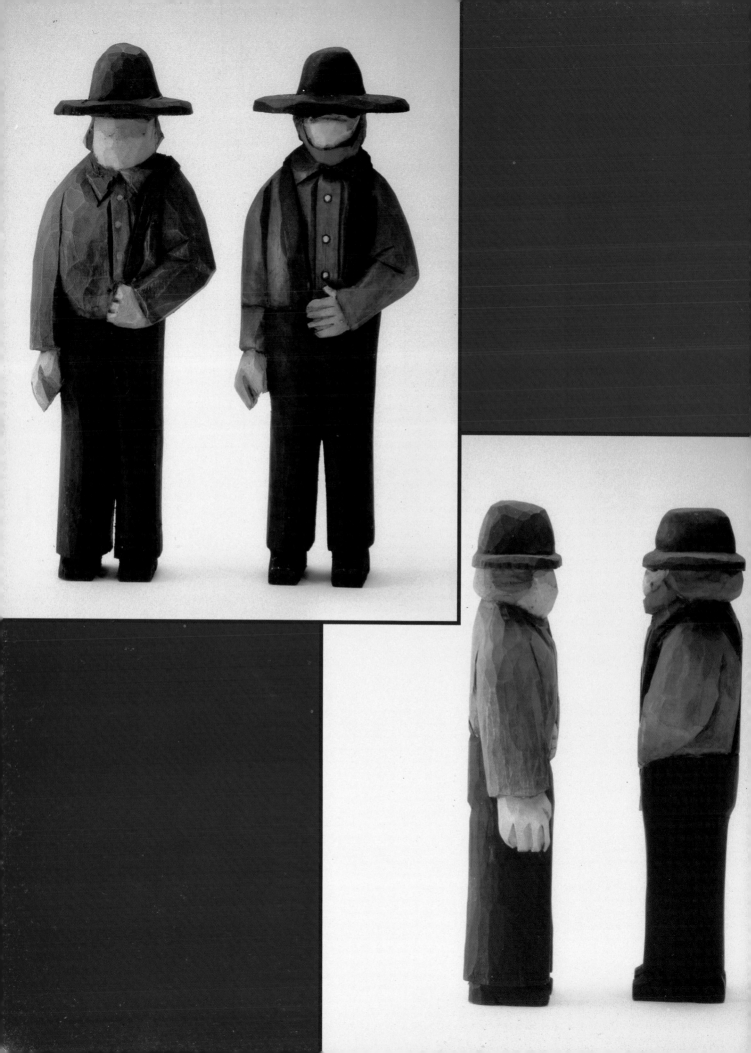

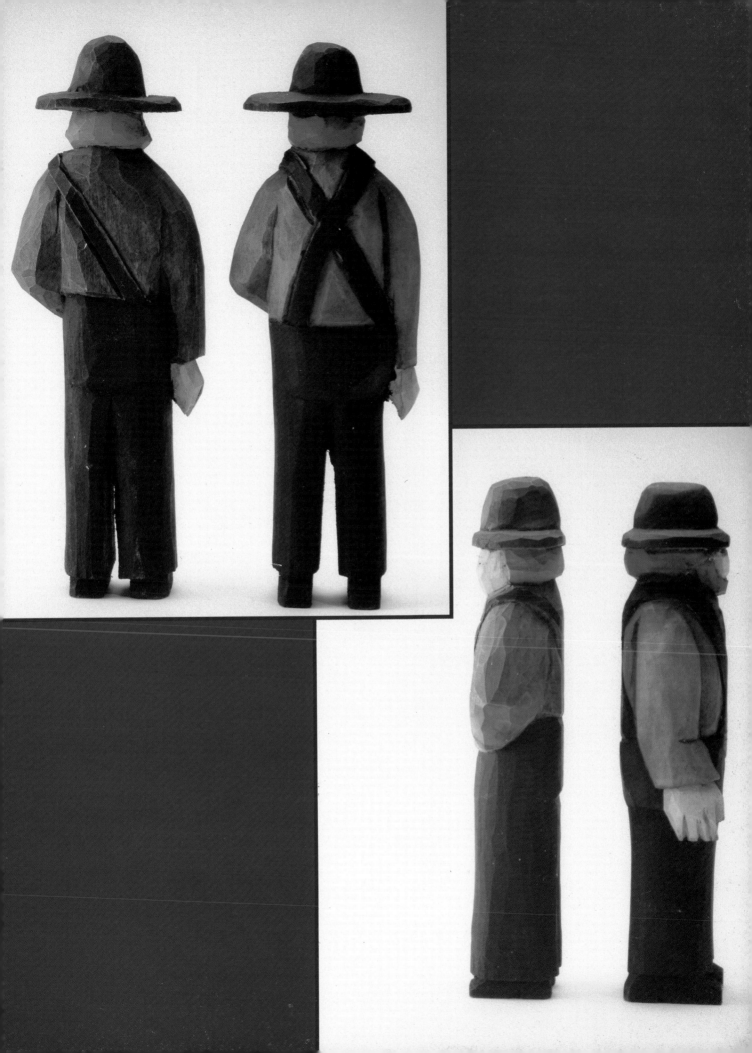

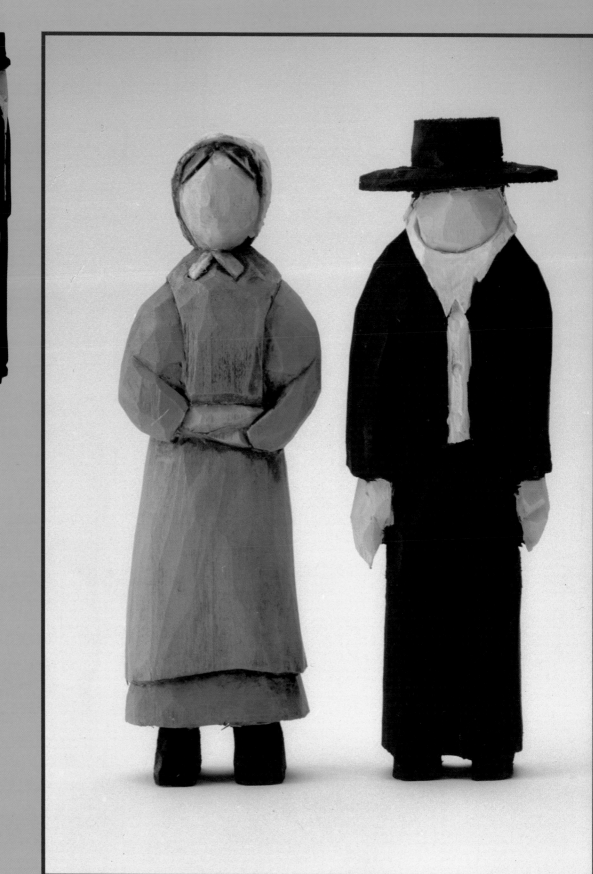